CREATING A RULE OF LIFE

A MANUAL FOR DANCING
TO DIVINE RHYTHMS

CREATING A RULE OF LIFE

A MANUAL FOR DANCING TO DIVINE RHYTHMS

JEAN WISE

"And those who were seen dancing were thought to be insane by those who could not hear the music."

- Friedrich Nietzsche

HEALTHY SPIRITUALITY PUBLISHING

Copyright © 2024 by Jean Wise.
ISBN:

All rights reserved. No part of this publication may be reproduced, distributed or transmitted in any form or by any means, including photocopying, recording, or other electronic or mechanical methods, without the prior written permission of the publisher, except in the case of brief quotations embodied in critical reviews and certain other noncommercial uses permitted by copyright law. For permission requests, write to the publisher, addressed "Attention: Permissions Coordinator," at the address below.
Healthy Spirituality Publishing Edon Ohio www.healthyspirituality.org

All Scripture quotations, unless otherwise indicated, are taken from the Holy Bible, New International Version®, NIV®. Copyright ©1973, 1978, 1984, 2011 by Biblica, Inc.TM Used by permission of Zondervan. All rights reserved worldwide. www.zondervan.com The "NIV" and "New International Version" are trademarks registered in the United States Patent and Trademark Office by Biblica, Inc.

Scripture quotations marked MSG are taken from *The Message*, copyright © 1993, 2002, 2018 by Eugene H. Peterson. Used by permission of NavPress. All rights reserved. Represented by Tyndale House Publishers.

DEDICATION

To those who came before us, creating and sharing their rule of life and
their divine dance routines.

To those we accompany now in our spiritual journey,
twirling together to God's rhythms.

To those who may read our rules later and
be inspired to create and share with the next generation
their own steps in this miraculous mirrored movement with God.

I sometimes forget
that I was created for Joy.
My mind is too busy.
My heart is too heavy
for me to remember
that I have been
Called to dance
the sacred dance of life.
I was created to smile.
To Love.
To be lifted up
and lift up others.
O' Sacred One
untangle my feet
from all that ensnares.
Free my soul
that we might
Dance
And that our dancing
might be contagious.

Hafiz

TABLE OF CONTENTS

INTRODUCTION		9
CHAPTER 1:	THE PRACTICE HALL	13
CHAPTER 2:	PREPARATION FOR A RULE OF LIFE	19
CHAPTER 3:	THE PURPOSE	27
CHAPTER 4:	PICK A STYLE	33
CHAPTER 5:	PICK A ROUTINE	45
CHAPTER 6:	PATTERNS OF CHOREOGRAPHY	55
CHAPTER 7:	DIVINE DANCE PARTNER	65
CHAPTER 8:	PRACTICE	75
RESOURCES		85
ABOUT THE AUTHOR		87

INTRODUCTION

"How do you get to Carnegie Hall?"
"Practice, practice, practice."

This joke has existed for years. Ask about how to get to Carnegie Hall and people know the answer. The response is humorous, as usually the person asking the question is seeking exact directions to find a physical location. The response is correct because there is a process, hours of preparation and training, and behind the scene drills and work to make it as an artist at Carnegie Hall.

As a spiritual director and a person of faith on her own spiritual journey, I hear others ask questions about how to discover a deeper experience of God. This is a question lingering in my own soul too. How do we all grow in our faith?

"How do you get closer to God? How do we grow in faith?"
"Practice, practice, practice."

Does practice, practice, practice work for spiritual growth? How can we build spiritual disciplines into our daily lives? Can we follow God's movements as we respond to his invitation to dance with him in the rhythms of life?

I don't believe spiritual formation happens through striving for perfection, putting on a good front for God, or blindly following rituals for purification to please a far-away God.

God is always present with us, closer than we can imagine. Our practices, our spiritual disciplines, don't make God come to us. God is already here. The Spirit nudges us closer, inviting us to listen and follow God's lead. These patterns and rhythms slow us down, open the ears of our hearts, and realign us with God's presence. Faith practices become the processes God uses to shape us. God is the Artist, the Potter. We are the clay.

> *"I cannot cause light; the most I can do is try to put myself in the path of its beam."*
> Annie Dillard

Creating your own rule of life provides a framework for fostering your relationship with God. The disciplines of prayer, worship, reading, and serving are examples of routines associated with divine rhythm. The practices that draw us in, the ones that stretch and shape us, the regular return and repetition, and the restart once again in this daily sacred rhythm, create a dance with God in a priceless intimacy.

Doesn't divine rhythm sound inviting? A rule of life isn't a mandate of harsh perfectionist requirements. Instead, we listen to the sacred music within us, then join into God's transforming movements within each day.

Come to the Divine Dance. Our Instructor awaits to teach us the routines and rhythms of sacred choreography found in a rule of life. Our job is to enter into the dance conservatory, learn the steps and patterns, and follow the Teacher, mirroring each step.

And don't forget this action. We must:

Practice, practice, practice.

Dancing with the Questions
1. What do you know about the rule of life spiritual practice?
2. Describe the invitation and curiosity you have about this faith practice.
3. Name one step you want to learn in the exploration of discovering divine rhythms in the rule of life.

Prayer
Thank you, Lord, for inviting me to dance with you. Help me learn each step and follow your ways so we can flow together in sacred rhythms. Amen

CHAPTER 1:
THE PRACTICE HALL

What fun it is to experience the energy and excitement found in dance routines we frequently see at wedding receptions.

The lights dim. The disc jockey asks for all eyes to turn to the entranceway. Music erupts as the bridal party is introduced. Each couple enters the room, rocking and rolling to their favorite beat, often showcasing intricate and well-rehearsed dance steps. Carefree joy surrounds the moment.

Later in the evening, the father-daughter dance or the mother-son dance starts slow with standard expectations, and then the music changes and they perform at an electrifying and entertaining professional level. We can almost see Fred Astaire and Ginger Rodgers on the dance floor before us. Joy fills the room. The dance becomes a gift for family and friends, given and received.

My granddaughter takes dance lessons. She goes to class every Monday, week after week, preparing for the last performance scheduled for spring. For a set period of time, she focuses on listening intently to the instructor, following every move. In fact, mirrors line a long wall so all the dancers can match the leader step by step.

Performance takes practice, preparation, and purpose.

We too are practicing, learning, becoming whole throughout our lives. God shapes our hearts as we return to God's creative presence. We can let our growth be haphazard and reactive to the stresses, demands, and interruptions in life, or we can approach each day with intention and purpose. A rule of life provides a framework for a meaningful life.

This book is about creating a rule of life. The tagline for this book is "Dancing to Divine Rhythms" and it is my hope that together we focus more on the word rhythm than the rigid connotations in the word "rule." God invites us to mirror the sacred rhythms in the divine dance. Where do we start?

Entering the Dance Conservatory

Writing and living within a rule for life is a spiritual practice leading to healthy spirituality. The first step in learning to dance and live within a rule of life is to enter the room of God. God's dance studio is open and ready for students to learn, practice, and shine. We know we are not perfect and will fail many times, but our call is to enter the hall and keep dancing.

Beginning a new spiritual practice takes courage and curiosity. When I go to a new place—a restaurant, a school, a new job—I am nervous and a little frightened. What will people expect from me? Will I fit in? Look like a fool? Fall on my face? Say or do the wrong thing?

I may not even know what door to enter. I have learned when a new person comes to our church to explain to them which door will be open. Often on weekdays, we lock the main sanctuary door and most people enter either through the south door facing the park or the one by the garage and kitchen just off the parking lot.

Then I try to meet them at the door, welcoming them into the building. I offer to show them around, especially where we will meet and, of course, where the restrooms are located. If we are meeting with a group, we begin with small talk to get to know each other better before easing into the agenda.

When I am the new person, or one trying a new spiritual practice, I take a deep breath and pray to be brave enough to enter this strange world.

I am grateful, knowing God will meet me at this new threshold and welcome me in. God desires us to draw closer to the sacred. To dance with the Divine. God will wait till we are ready, encourage us to begin, and gently teach us how to dance.

Writing a rule of life begins with prayer. Ask God to guide you in this practice. My prayer at first is for courage and curiosity. I share with God my hesitation about this unknown. I enter prayer with open hands and a willing heart to listen and learn.

I confess I really don't know what I am doing. I know I need to learn, stay open to ideas, and be flexible in revision. Remember, a rule of life is a living document that changes and grows as you do. Each year, and often several times within a year, I find a new word, insight, or quote to add to my ever-evolving rule.

The best rule of life is one that is your own, created in alignment with how God is calling you to live your life. Your first step begins with prayerful reflection, open to the discovery of elements resonating in your heart and matching what God plants in your soul. You start a bit unsure and give words to God's shaping and imagining.

Set some time aside to talk and listen to God about a rule of life. Journal your prayers. Articulate your desire to receive the gift of sacred rhythms to frame your walk with God.

Starting a new spiritual practice can be exciting and life-giving while a bit terrifying. We wonder if we will "succeed," quit too soon, find it too difficult or uncomfortable. What if we don't do "it" right?

Ask God for courage to take that first step in learning more about a rule of life. Request a taste of wonder and curiosity about what it could mean for your spiritual walk. God is good and will give you just what you need for this season of your life.

Mary Oliver writes in her poem titled "Sometimes:"

> *"Instructions for living a life:*
> *Pay attention.*
> *Be astonished.*
> *Tell about it."*

This is great advice for beginning this new spiritual practice, for entering the dance hall to learn.

Pay attention. Be ready to observe and learn. Be open to new ideas and trying something new and unfamiliar. Adopt a beginner's mind, thirsty to discover new rhythms. What are others saying about writing a rule of life?

Be astonished. Just as the fancy dances of the bridal party at wedding receptions captivate our surprise and wonder, coming closer to God in prayer, reminds us of God's power, grace, and invitation to draw near. Be honest in your desire to learn more. Hold your hands open to receive whatever surprise God sends.

Tell about it. Ask others about their rule of life. Not just what they wrote or how they practice, be curious about what led them to establish this practice. What helped them along the way in discovering what worked and what didn't work. Share your growing desire to develop a rule of life with someone you trust and talk about what will help you begin this process.

Enter the practice hall, the dance conservatory, and look around. God will welcome you in.

Dancing with Questions

1. Remember a time you first entered a strange new place? Recall the emotions and what helped you feel more at home.
2. Imagine God welcoming you to come closer. What are the words God says to your heart? How do you respond?
3. Where do you need courage and curiosity to begin this new practice?

Prayer

Lord, I am not sure at all what I am doing. Where to start? How to begin? Thank you for welcoming me into this new place and I ask for an open heart and mind to learn the things you desire of me. Amen

CHAPTER 2:
PREPARATION FOR A RULE OF LIFE

Most of us already follow some type of unspoken rules each day. We brush our teeth and drink coffee every morning. We don't leave the driveway until everyone in the car buckles their seatbelt. I kiss my hubby goodbye when he leaves the house, and he calls his mother every Sunday. I firmly believe in going on a retreat at least once a year and try to write in my journal regularly. At the end of each day, I ask myself, what am I most grateful for this past day?

We act without thinking to look both ways before crossing the street. Our parents may have taught us to always say please and thank you. Some families have specific rules, particular only to them, such as don't put the ketchup bottle on the Thanksgiving table. (Yes, we followed that silly one at the home where I grew up.)

Our lives contain rules, guidelines, and rhythms, and we aren't aware of how they frame our actions and behaviors. Yet they exist and influence our daily lives.

Whether or not we verbalize rules, we are already living by basic tenets. These internal and often unconscious regulations may be intentional or instinctive, but they form our habits and guide how we approach life.

Very few people have a conscious plan for developing their spiritual lives. Most Christians are not intentional, but operate more on autopilot. When we open our hearts to God and ask for guidance and clarity for a personal rule of life, purpose flourishes in our lives.

Writing your spiritual rules is an intentional and powerful practice. Living within a rule for life leads to vibrant, healthy spirituality.

What is a Rule of Life?
A rule for life is a collection of guidelines for living. It can also be called a "way of life." Its purpose is to help us keep our sense of balance by intentionally addressing all aspects of life: physical, emotional, socially, spiritually, etc.

A rule of life is a plan to keep our hearts and minds centered on God, knowing that God is the source of all life. We focus on spiritual practices that provide a framework to support living how God calls us to live and be with God.

A rule of life reminds us who God is and who we are as his beloved children. These simple guidelines help us pay attention to God's presence in our moments and to see his loving touch in our lives.

> *"The Latin word for 'rule' is 'regula" from which our words 'regular' and 'regulate' derive. A rule of life is not meant to be restrictive, although it certainly asks for genuine commitment. It is meant to help us establish a rhythm of daily living . . . a rule of life, like a trellis, curbs our tendency to wander and supports our frail efforts to grow spiritually."*
> Marjorie Thompson

In Greek, one meaning of the word "rule" is trellis. What a wonderful image that gives us. In the garden or vineyard, a trellis supports the branches in their growth upward and outward, helping to produce a bountiful harvest. Likewise, the trellis of a rule of life enables us to abide in God with a fruitful spiritual life.

A rule of life provides the essential framework for our journey with God. As Adele Calhoun says, "Life-giving rules are a brief and realistic scaffold of disciplines that support your heart's desire to grow in loving God and others."

A rule is a regular rhythm we choose for our life in order to focus more on the ways of God. Through a rule, we partner with God's transforming work in our lives. A rule of life gives us priorities and direction. It serves to weed out things that do not lead us closer to God. It is an intentional way of thinking about your own spiritual journey and how you are growing to become more like Christ.

> *"A rule of life, very simply, is an intentional, conscious plan to keep God at the center of everything we do . . . The starting point and foundation of any rule is a desire to be with God and to love him."*
> *Peter Scazzero*

A rule of life is not a set of New Year's resolutions or goals for the coming year. A rule of life is simply statements that guide your life, a manifesto, a collection of values and actions you want to adopt to live faithfully.

These guidelines reflect our ideal values. Instead of being reactive to the urgent, the disruptive, the distractions of daily living, we find strength on the foundation of practices that remind us how we want to live: not a life scattered and shattered, but even in dark times, a life centered on God.

When I first began to write this book we were in the middle of the Covid pandemic. Already our patience was strained, and uncertainty surrounded us as we did not know how long this transformative, out-of-control event would last. Looking back now, that whole experience lasted longer than most predicted and still has an effect on our lives today. Covid shook our existence and forced many of us into a new perspective of life. Having a clearly stated foundation in my rule of life grounded me and provided a solid footing amidst a shaky environment.

A rule of life cultivated with God keeps our life focused on God and opens our hearts to be nurtured by his grace and love. Our deepest desires determine our rule of life within and with God's desires for our life.

Each of us can create a unique rule for life. We can fill up an entire page with statements or we can write a simple one sentence statement of beliefs. The foundation to consider is this: how can I be open to the Holy Spirit and grow closer to God?

Remember a rule of life isn't the law or imposition of regulations mandating a perfect life. These are gentle boundaries of how we want to live and help us stay on the path where God leads us.

They are not the "musts", but aspirations we desire to aim for in our daily lives. A rule of life is not constrictive but permissive. It creates an environment to live with purpose and clear intentions.

The idea is to find patterns that work for you, pick particular styles and practices, try them out until you find the rhythms and patterns that best draw you to God. Remember we first partner with God, following his lead, mirroring his movements.

I appreciate how Richard Foster expresses this idea. "A farmer is helpless to grow grain; all he can do is provide the right conditions for the growing of grain . . . This is the way it is with the spiritual disciplines – they are a way of sowing to the Spirit. . . By themselves the spiritual disciplines can do nothing; they can only get us to the place where something can be done."

In the divine dance, we match God's movements. The divine dancing with us. A rhythm is a recurring pattern. Instead of dwelling on the rigidity of the word "rule", the image of dancing with God, mirroring the movements in our lives, gives us a welcoming way of living.

As part of my training as a spiritual director ten years ago, we were encouraged to write our rule of life. I keep a copy of my rule in my journal and my Bible and often look at its wisdom. Am I adhering to my basic beliefs and do my thoughts and behavior mirror them? Over the years, I have revised them, but amazingly, they are quite similar to what I originally wrote. I find having a rule of life helps me refocus on my deepest desire – to be with God, learn to love like God, and to serve God as I am called.

My human heart fails many, many times to follow these rules, but they give me guidance, call me back to my core beliefs, and help me refocus my desires on God when the world and sin distract me.

I recently revised my rule as it continues to develop and nourish my spirituality. I have a friend who wrote a longer rule for herself one year, then condensed it to four sentences as she applied it to her daily living.

Quite a few years ago, I took a nursing career planning course. One activity was to write out by hand what our ideal job would look like. I struggled to discern what I wanted to do as a nurse and where God was calling me in this profession. I remember not being too excited about this imaginary game, but I did the assignment anyway, and put the paper away.

Surprisingly, five years later I stumbled upon the wrinkled scrap of paper that describe pretty darn close the work I was actually doing at that time. Most of my work at a local health department matched what I imagined years before. Writing out how you want to live and be with God is transformational.

Writing out our deepest desires and how we want to live as a child of God is powerful. Instead of tackling each day, each season of our life haphazardly and reactive, we clarify and follow the patterns, the rhythms of life. How do I want to live? What is God's calling me to be like? How can I arrange my life to hear God and dance with God?

> *"I will instruct you and teach you the way you should go;*
> *I will counsel you with my eye upon you."*
> Psalm 32:8

Dancing with the Questions
1. What are some unspoken, unrecognized rules you already live by?
2. Have you found some resistance or hesitation in creating a rule of life?
3. Write out how it feels deep inside your heart when you imagine dancing with God?

Prayer
Start the music, Maestro, and let the dance begin. Teach me the foundations through the explorations of rules and rhythms and reveal its purpose in my life. Help me hear your wisdom and music. Amen.

CHAPTER 3:
THE PURPOSE

The purpose of a rule is to articulate working guidelines for our spiritual life and provide a framework for the balanced patterns of living, of dancing with God. Spiritual practices compose a rule, giving us margins and creating space in our hearts for God to abide.

> *"A rule provides creative boundaries that allow*
> *for the recognition and celebration of God's loving presence.*
> *It does not prescribe but invite, it does not force but guide,*
> *it does not threaten but warn, it does not instill fear but points to love.*
> *In this it is a call to freedom, freedom to love."*
> *Henri Nouwen*

Here are some benefits of taking the time to write a rule of life and then living by them:

- Conversion–A rule of life forms and transforms us. It helps us with life's ongoing and most essential questions: Who am I and how do I want to live? As we grow closer to God and live as God calls us, we continue to ask: How am I being guided by the divine and shaped into God's image?

- Clarity–Doing inner work provides clarity even in times of foggy confusion. A map helps us when we are lost.
- Consistency–Knowing our values and how we want to live helps establish routines that provide continual nourishment for our spirit. We can sense earlier if the "well" is beginning to run dry. Our rule also helps us stay accountable to our surrender/commitment to God.
- Calibrate–A rule of life sets us in the right direction and reminds us who God is, how he wants us to live and what God puts into our hearts. When we drift or get lost in the all the noise and confusion of the world, our rule calls us back to our core beliefs, and helps refocus our desires on God alone.

I love the image of how a rule of life calibrates my direction. I struggle to articulate how I deeply believe God wants me to live. I struggle to find the words and put them onto paper. Then I reread them regularly to realign myself with God, with my heart, and with my deepest yearnings.

A rule of life helps me remember and reconnect with my values. They serve as my anchor.

Remember these four key points as you prepare to discover your rule:

A rule of life emerges slowly. Most people don't jot one down quickly. They work out their own rule, bit by bit, for their own life's wants and desires.

Second, don't make a rule so perfect that it's unattainable. A rule describes the ideal, the wonderful possibilities in your spirituality with a hint to challenge and stretch you a little.

Third, a rule describes a framework, a pattern on how you want to live, especially in your experience of God. The rule shouldn't mandate or feel oppressive. A rule is better to be brief, open, and encouraging than authoritative and a burden.

Last, your rule names specific things you want to do to grow spiritually. Not just "to live a better life" but how that life might appear. What will you do? How often? When? Be specific.

Review the rule often. I like to visit my rule at the start of every year, then occasionally read it throughout the year. Your rule is always open for revision as needed and can be revisited even after a long absence.

All this preparation requires "inner work" on the heart and soul. What does that mean?

Inner work is the point where emotions, beliefs, and mindset intersect. Who are you at the deepest level? Where is the true self—the one who you really are, not what the world, your parents, or circumstances imposed upon you?

We cannot rush these deep questions. Hearing the voice of the Spirit who created you requires time, quiet, patience, and willingness to let go of old narratives and false beliefs. Courage is necessary to undertake the inner work, which will guide you in discovering how God wants you to live.

Being ready to do this inner work is an early step in preparation to identifying our rule of life.

> *"The purpose of the Rule of Life is to strengthen our abiding in Christ by bringing rhythm, discipline, and order to our discipleship. The Rule helps us offer the whole of ourselves to God each day and keeps us open to God's love and will for us."*
> David Vryhof

Brief History of the Rule of Life

We are not the first generation to explore living by a rule of life. The first Christians in Acts 2: 42 "devoted themselves to the apostles' teaching and to the fellowship, to the breaking of bread and to prayer." This rule describes the practices that shaped their individual and corporate spirituality. The rule offered practices that opened space for them to attend to God's presence in and among them. Practicing this rule set the early Christians apart from the rest of the culture in which they lived.

Rules for living also grew out of the monastic movement, helping the monks to grow spiritually while in community. Pachomius, who lived in Egypt between 292 and 346 AD, wrote the first known rules. Daily prayers were a foundation for his guidelines.

St Benedict from the 6th century wrote one of the best-known rules for life. His word provided a framework, a way of living that fostered spiritual growth individually and in communal life. His guide included rules for obedience, silence, humility, hospitality, prayer, and work.

Dancing with God invites us to mirror his steps in a beautiful rhythm in daily life. Like a child walking on top of her/his father's feet, we relax, flow, and find our true selves as we follow God's movement.

Enter God's dance conservatory and begin your lessons. You are prepared now and can understand the purpose and benefits of learning this dance, taking the first step in creating a rule of life.

> *"I prefer the language of rhythm because it speaks of regularity that the body and soul can count on, but it also speaks of ebb and flow, creativity and beauty, music and dancing, joy and giving ourselves over to a force or a power that is beyond ourselves and is deeply good. Over time, as we surrender ourselves to new life rhythms, they help us to surrender old behaviors, attitudes and practices so that we can be shaped by new ones."*
> Ruth Haley Barton

Dancing with the Questions

1. What are your "go-to" practices, the essential spiritual practices you now use?
2. Consider how often you enter God's presence and what helps and hinders this time with God?

3. Write out your conversation with God as you ask him to lead you in writing out a rule of life.

Prayer:

Lord, as I deepen my sense of what a rule of life is and how it may help form my life, help me hear your instructions. I want to live according to the pattern you have designed for me. Show me the way. Amen.

CHAPTER 4:
PICK A STYLE

Can you guess how many styles of dance exist?

Depending on who you ask and how to categorize them, the exact number varies from broad areas such as classic, jazz, and Latin to specific genre such as Hip-hop, polka, and belly dancing. Some styles we are familiar with, such as ballet and tap. Others originate from exotic places and carry odd names like ziganka (a Russian folk dance) and Affranchi (Haiti).

Each style offers different levels of skills, but all share the common goal of artistic expression. People choose what style appeals to them. They may also try a new form of dance for the challenge or to develop a new repertoire. Attempting a different form stretches new muscles and creates novel, fun experiences.

Dance is a learnable skill requiring intention and practice. This is also true about a life of faith. God has given us the ability to learn and invites us and guides us to keep growing in our faith.

What do I mean by picking a style for your rule of life? What do you need to be aware of and how do you begin this search?

As in dance preferences, creating a framework on how you want to nurture your faith and grow spiritually reflects personal styles and preferences. For some people, certain faith practices appeal more than others. Occasionally, we become very efficient in one type. Other times, we want to learn a new discipline to stir our souls or break us out of the rut of routine. One practice may suddenly resonate with us, almost inviting us to come take a twirl and learn the steps.

I know what essential faith practices come easily and serve as a foundation for my own spiritual health. I turn to these trusty basics, especially in times of stress. Prayer, worship, journaling, silence, and stillness all nourish my soul.

When I find myself restless, confused, overwhelmed or uncertain, I come back to practices that has given me life in my past. Ones that I return to often, enter with little effort, and know will restore my sense of spiritual balance.

Yet I love to learn new practices such as soul collage, creative lettering, or a new type of serving others. Trying out a new rule, like a new dance step, excites me. I feel its energy and enjoy its creativity. Like a fresh icy cup of water on a hot, parched day, new disciplines relieve my thirst and I experience life in new ways.

Where To Start?

Where do we start in picking a style to create a rule of life? Sometimes the sheer number of spiritual disciplines, ranging from simple to complex, distract us from finding the practice our soul desires.

Often I start reading what works for others, checking out how my favorite people of faith, past and current, fueled their faith. A word of caution: like bright shiny objects, we often jump from one idea to another without pausing to discern where God is leading us in our faith and what we know we deeply need.

Always start with prayer and listening to God.

Something else to consider is this: different seasons of life influence what spiritual practices best nurture our souls at that time. Name where you are in life, right now.

A busy parent with young children? A caregiver for a loved one? Recovering from an illness, surgery, or injury? In a life transition such as retirement, a move, or a major change in family? Be aware that any time you face discernment, change, or uncertainty is a good time to review and assess your rule of life.

Identifying your season in life will provide insight into picking a style.

What is your deepest desire? Pray. Articulate that desire. Knowing what you deeply yearn for can guide you. The practice of journaling and talking with a spiritual director may help you find and name that longing in your heart.

Remember when picking a style, you may need to go back to the basics, returning to disciplines that brought you comfort and peace. Or maybe your spirit is thirsty to try a new way of experiencing God. Listen deeply to what you need at this present moment.

Knowing a few steps before you write out the specifics of your rule offers a sense of direction in this exploration of where God is calling you to grow.

Four Steps of Discovering Styles

The four steps to discover your style are:
1. Be personal
2. Be attentive
3. Be intentional
4. Be pliable

Be Personal

The first step is knowing yourself and your prayer preferences. Personally, I love silence and the quiet times with God. The best practices for the foundation of my rule of life are devotionals, Bible reading, journaling, contemplative prayer, and silent retreats.

One of my friends experienced restlessness and discomfort at the silent retreat we attended together. She said later, though she appreciated the resting and spiritual time with God, she heard the Lord better when she walked in her woods or served communion at church. Interacting in small groups, sharing her faith, and listening to others' stories of God are things she loves. She nourishes her spirit in a different way than I do.

We are all unique children of God, and our rule of life will vary from person to person. Keep this in mind as you discern the framework of your rule. And always, place this process into God's hands, asking for guidance, an open heart, and clarity to hear his direction.

Step one is knowing your personal preferences and considering your current phase of life. Take time to write out what best draws you closer to God and what new practices you could try at some point in your life.

Be Attentive

The second step is paying attention. Ask yourself how you experienced God in the past and how you hear him currently. What brings you joy? Comfort? Guidance? You may also be feeling a curiosity, an invitation for a new practice. Listen for God's leading, his nudge in creating a rule of life.

Take the time to reflect and remember what practices nurtured your spirit across your lifetime. What disciplines were life-giving to you? Name the essential rituals and routines that brought you joy, peace, comfort, strength. Which ones helped you to know and experience God?

Be attentive to your current hunger and need for God. What is missing right now in your relationship with the Lord? What practice are you rejecting immediately? Take a few minutes to ponder why you are resistant to that discipline.

Talk with God and ask for help in observing what has worked for you in the past, what you need right now, and where he might be leading you to grow.

Ruth Haley Barton, in her book Sacred Rhythms, shared these questions to challenge us for consideration:

How bad do I want these deep desires/longings for God?

- Am I willing to rearrange my life for what my heart most wants?
- Which spiritual practices and relationships have seemed to be most powerful in meeting the desires of my heart?
- What am I beginning to understand about my minimum daily/weekly/monthly requirements for ongoing spiritual formation?
- Which disciplines do I know I need to engage in regularly as a way of offering myself to God steadily and consistently?

I like the questions Marjorie Thompson writes in Soul Feast for reflection too:

What am I deeply attracted to, and why?
Where do I feel God is calling me to stretch and grow?
What kind of balance do I need in my life?

Additional questions to ponder:

- What kind of person is God inviting you to be?

- What practices in the past drew you closer to God and you find a natural affinity toward? Write all the practices that resonate with you and that you find attractive.
- What practices have you avoided that may have led to a gap in your spirituality? Talk with God about your resistance to some of these ideas and be open to adding a few to your rule.
- How could your rule nourish you in head, heart, and hands?
- How is your rule balanced in physical, mental, emotional, financial, and spiritual arenas?
- Do your rules contain elements of individual and community activity?

Using questions like these helps me find the words I can't quite express and often identifies my deepest need. If one question resonates within me, stirs my spirit, I write that one out in my journal and talk with God. I wonder why that specific question spoke to me. I keep the question in mind for several days, even weeks, listening for clues to its lessons.

Be Intentional

The third step in discovering styles to match a rule of life is to be intentional. Think balance when you review what practices you may include in your framework. What is missing?

I am an introvert and as I began composing my rule of life, I noticed community, service, and hospitality were missing. I knew the quieter practices came easier and were more natural to my personality.

Yet in all honestly, balance leads to a whole, healthier spirituality. I listed hospitality, then took this practice to God, asking that he show me what I needed to learn and how to grow deeper.

Hospitality continues to be listed in my rule and with each year, I learn new insights from its practice. I am grateful that God nudged me to seek balance and that he continues to form this unnatural tendency within my heart.

Debra Farrington lists eight areas to consider when gathering ideas and balancing the foundation of our rule. In her book, Living Faith Day by Day, she encourages us to pick a practice under each of the following areas:

1. Foundations (putting God at the center of your rule and your life)
2. Prayer (finding a prayer type and rhythm that works for you)
3. Work (approaching your work as part of your spiritual life rather than something divorced from it)
4. Study (establishing a regular practice of learning more about God)
5. Spiritual companionship (committing yourself to regular companionship and community on the journey)
6. Care of your body (taking care of yourself as a spiritual practice)
7. Reaching out (caring for others and the environment as a spiritual practice)
8. Hospitality (finding ways to be a gracious presence in the world)

Jesus followed essential patterns for his life, too. In the Bible, we see him praying, studying and sharing the scriptures, serving others, listening, healing, and seeking quiet times with God. He fasted. He worshipped.

Jesus' practices stretch our faith too when we witness how he gave his life for others with love and forgiveness. Choosing love over anger and despair is one discipline that was not originally written in my rule, but was added as I grew in my faith. Studying Jesus' life and how he lived each day will clarify the framework of how we too shall live.

Be Pliable

The last step to consider in discerning a style for a rule of life is to be pliable. What you initially write out won't be your final rule. Rules of life continue to evolve and grow with you and your experiences. Be willing to let go of some ideas and be open to receive others. Be flexible; holding lightly to your rule, always offering it back to God for his blessing.

Writing and living within a rule of life is a spiritual practice that can help lead to healthy spirituality. Naming the patterns like different dance categories help me hear God's guidance as I write and update my rule. Pick a pattern and start dancing!

Dancing with the Questions

1. Prayerfully read the following reflection and notice patterns and rhythms of what sustains you and what feeds your desire to grow. What practices resonate in your spirit and help realign your daily life?

> Imagine it is five years from now and we meet for coffee. I ask you, how is your soul?
> You answer, "All is well. Actually, I am in a really good place in all areas of life right now."
> Tell me why your life is so amazing in this scene. Describe it. What does it look like? Can you tell me what you're doing? What practices are you engaged with? How is it balanced and fulfilling? Describe your ideal day.

2. Choose one or several of the questions (there are many!) listed in this chapter. Here are some examples:

   - What kind of balance do I need in my life?
   - Am I in a more stable time to experiment with a new practice? Or do I need the stability of well-known ways of God?
   - Where do I feel God is calling me to stretch and grow?
   - What am I beginning to understand about my minimum daily/weekly/monthly requirements for ongoing spiritual formation?
   - What practices have I avoided that may have led to a gap in my spirituality?
   - How could my rule nourish me in head, heart, and hands?

3. What did you notice or learn that will influence how you write your rule?

Prayer

Lord, I am just learning to dance with you in your divine rhythm. Show me the patterns that match my soul. Reveal the practices that I need in good times and in difficult times to open my heart and draw closer to you. Thank you for your guidance. Amen.

CHAPTER 5:
PICK A ROUTINE

"Take your every day, ordinary life—your sleeping, eating, going-to-work, and walking around life—and place it before God as an offering. Embracing what God does for you is the best thing you can do for him. Don't become so well adjusted to our culture that you fit into it without even thinking. Instead, fix your attention on God. You'll be changed from the inside out."
Romans 12:1-3 The Message

Dancers don't instantly perform the perfect dance. They slowly build the sequence of movements, one step at a time. Dancers arrange one segment or interval of flow and music with and within others.

Dancers learn one portion of a new show, then gradually combine and connect the sections until the final product is complete.

We create our rule of life in the same fashion. Discovering and exploring the different broad categories that make our framework is the next step in this process. We, like dancers, discover and explore the building blocks of our rule of life.

Imagine you have before you a 1000-piece puzzle. Some people start by finding all the edge pieces and frame the future picture. Others like to first compile like-colored pieces and begin connecting several segments of the picture in different piles. You best know your preference to avoid the overwhelming confusion a new project presents and how to keep focused on a complete and personalized work of art/your rule of life.

This chapter will give you tips on narrowing down the broad decisions on what to include in your rule of life and then give you categories to consider with some examples for inspiration.

8 Tips for Writing a Rule of Life

Immerse this whole practice from start to ongoing in prayer. Remember a rule of life is a gift from God. Be open to receive his offerings. As you identify general categories, converse with God, asking if different ones bring peace, joy, and love. At this current time, does this idea bring you closer to God?

1. Pray, listen, read, go deep—allow the words of your own rule to slowly emerge from deep within your soul. Create time and space for it to bud and blossom. Block off time on your calendar for this project. Go on retreat, spending time just being with God, listening for his guidance. Write something initially and let it brew to full flavor. Begin an idea journal to gather thoughts. Listening and simmering are all part of the process.

2. Identify your key priorities in life. The questions from the last chapter will guide this process. Research the internet for a core value identification exercise. Often these worksheets list 50-100 examples of important human traits and, reading through them, circle those that resonate with your spirit. Then you have to narrow your list to a smaller number. This can be difficult but insightful for what really matters to your soul.
3. Spend some time thinking about what spiritual practices draw you closer to God. What spiritual disciplines is God inviting you to try? Think of it as an inventory of how you nurture a healthy spirituality for yourself. Another fun image is to imagine what is in your spiritual toolbox. Think about a project that requires different tools: some you use all the time, such as a hammer or screwdriver; others you use only occasionally or for a special project.
4. Think about your season of life and your daily demands on your time. Pay attention to your life right now. How do your priorities and essential practices currently align with your life? What is realistic?
5. Describe your sense of balance for all the dimensions of your life. Your relationships. Your work. Your joy. Your self-care. Your finances. What needs to be cultivated and what needs to be weeded from how you work and live? Be honest, where do you waste time? What do you need to release and let go of in order to rest, learn, grow, and live as God is calling you to do?
6. Write your rule of life in positive, affirming, already occurring sentences such as I begin each day with prayer

and reading devotions. I exercise daily. Once a year, I attend a silent retreat. I honor the Sabbath each week for rest and to worship God. I found it powerful to use "I am" sentences. I am a child of God. I am a writer. I am a contemplative. I am creative.

7. Remember to keep your rule simple and realistic, yet challenging enough to stretch you to grow. This often comes later after you have written, used, and tried on your rule for a period. Dancers often revise steps once they put the whole routine together. A rule of life will evolve as well.
8. Too often we focus on the "rule" and forget the word "life." What gives you life? How do you like to live? What is your ideal life?

GLOWS

One more way to consider as you begin this adventure is this: a rule of life GLOWS:

G–stands for God. Keep God front and center. God is the focal point of the rules and focusing on him first will add balance to your life. Another G word is general. Remember your rule is general enough to serve as a framework, yet specific enough to give you guidance for your spiritual life.

L–Lifegiving. When you read your rule, it energizes and excites you, rather than seeing it as a burden. As Adele Calhoun says, "Life-giving rules are a brief and realistic scaffold of disciplines that support your heart's desire to grow in loving God and others." A rule addresses your relationship with God, other people, and the world. Your rule is for your unique spiritual formation and not for comparing your life and spirituality to someone else's path in life.

<u>O–Obtainable and realistic</u>. Rules are simple and sustainable rather than complex and unworkable. Don't get too complex or try to create the perfect rule.

<u>W–full of wisdom and wonder</u>. Your rule inspires, stretches, and encourages you. A rule of life is uniquely yours and may take time to develop. Wisdom to feed your mind and wonder to fill your heart. Add a touch of whimsey to remind you of God's joy and love.

<u>S–Feeds your spirit.</u> Your rule nourishes your soul and draws you closer to God and fosters spiritual growth. A rule refreshes the soul and nourishes life.

Organize your rule by time: daily, weekly, monthly, yearly, every five years. Personally, I use regularly and occasionally instead of more rigid daily and weekly. Some people will define the word "regularly" meaning daily or weekly. Occasionally could be quarterly or as needed. Know how you are using these words.

Play with combining some areas or reducing them under one umbrella. You may reduce the categories to three major themes such as internal or inward, friends/family or outward, your outreach to others and community, or how your practices interweave with others.

Another grouping could be physical, mental, and spiritual.

Once I recorded on paper what I felt best drawn to for my rule of life, the pattern or organization didn't matter to me. My only pattern is to keep them to one page and have a silly rule that the more important ones to my spiritual growth are "above the fold," the top half of my one-page sheet.

> *"Your way of acting should differ from the world's way. The love of Christ must come before all else."*
> St Benedict

Examples of Rules

I gathered some examples of rule of life. Some of the following are not the complete rules, but will give you a sample of ideas to consider.

I will strive to:

- Seek, know, serve, and love God with all my heart, mind, and soul.
- Nurture others and myself in a deepening relationship with God.
- Meditate more on the love of God rather than our love for Him (Theresa of Avila). He, not me.
- Intentionally fix my eyes on Jesus as the author and perfecter of my faith. (Hebrews 12:2)
- Open myself up daily to the work and presence of the Holy Spirit as an advocate, teacher, director, companion, and friend. He is my source of wisdom and might.
- Be obedient to God's Word and Will, be discerning of His will and be open to the work God is doing within me. My prayer is: Do what You need to do in order that I become what You best choose for me.

- Pray continuously, working more on listening than babbling my perceived needs to God.
- Recognize all that I have is from God and for God, and in reality, I possess nothing. <u>God is enough</u>. Intentionally sit quietly to contemplate God.
- Follow the mind and heart of Jesus by thinking of things that are true, noble, right, pure, lovely, admirable, excellent, and praiseworthy (Philippians 4:8)
- Daily examen—what am I most grateful for and what am I least grateful for and hold these both lightly.
- Practice the spiritual disciplines of prayer, study, worship, fasting, meditation, simplicity, journal writing, solitude, submission, service, focus (stability), guidance, and celebration in an intentional and integrated way.
- Be committed to exercise and better nutrition for my body.
- Practice stewardship with stuff; money, time, and relationships. I have enough.
- Be gentle with myself and love and accept the person God created me to be. I am a beloved child of God.

Here is another approach to collecting patterns to organize your rule. You could start with broad categories such as grow, connect, support, and serve as this example from the "Community of the Gospel:"

Grow
Daily prayer.
Collect and use books of personal devotions.
Commit to regular, intentional prayer times for rhythm of life.

Try different approaches to prayer, such as centering prayer, the Daily Office, meditation, contemplative prayer. Join a prayer group or chain, praying for the needs of others.

Study of scripture and spiritual writings

Participate in Bible study and adult formation classes and groups.

Quiet time.

Connect

Seek Christ in all persons.

Love my neighbor as myself.

Proclaim Christ through the ministry of hospitality: welcome and acceptance.

Be totally present for others.

Practice kindness and restraint in all situations.

Support

Learn to see Christ in others.

Be trustworthy and kind toward each other.

Walk with one another through life's griefs, joys, thanksgivings, anxieties, needs, and dry spells.

Serve one another as a source of courage and strength.

Serve

Proclaim Christ through good works and acts of charity.

Search out the holy in everyday tasks and duties.

Commit some time, talent, and resources as a grateful response to God's love.

Care for the environment, God's creation.

Assume servant leadership in church and community.

Educate about issues related to peace, justice, and dignity.

Other ideas could be:

- Saying morning prayer every day.
- Daily prayers of intercession for those in need.
- Singing in the choir.
- Engaging in spiritual direction.
- Participate regularly in the worship, study and work of the church.
- Get adequate rest during each day and at night, and balance work activities with intentionally chosen personal and family recreation.
- Assess frequently if mindless activities such as games, phone, or computer are a distraction from what matters.
- Don't speak badly, gossip, or malign others.
- Manage money and time well.
- Make time for reflection daily.

The ideas are endless. Remember the purpose of this chapter is to gather possibilities and begin grouping them together. If a particular practice interests you but just doesn't fit, pray about it. Spend some time finding the right word to describe what you are seeking when you first read that idea.

Dancing with the Questions

1. What practices do you find in the Bible that Jesus frequently practiced?
2. Imagine a large garden basket and you are walking through the garden with God gathering just the right arrangement

for your table. Review the ideas in this chapter with that image in mind.
3. Remember this is a rule of LIFE. What gives you life? How do you like to live? How do you feel God is inviting you closer? What is your ideal life?

Prayer

Lord, I open to your leading as I gather ideas for my rule of life and listen to your wisdom on how to find the best ones to help me grow. I know learning these patterns will bring me closer to you and help me live as you have created me to be. Amen.

CHAPTER 6:
PATTERNS OF CHOREOGRAPHY

"Then Miriam the prophet, Aaron's sister, took a timbrel in her hand, and all the women followed her, with timbrels and dancing."
Exodus 15: 20, NIV

Miriam, Aaron's sister, knew the patterns. She knew just when to begin to dance, when the timing was right to rejoice and add lively movements to each step. She packed her timbrels ahead of time, so she was ready when the time was right. She paid attention and listened. She followed. She danced when God said, "It's time."

Deep listening to God as our Choreographer enriches us with creative ideas. We are surrounded by his perfect arrangement and swells within our spiritual movements that we never imagined.

Last chapter we gathered ideas, pieces of the dance. Now, how do these movements flow together? How will you organize your rule of life, so it blends with the rhythms in your life journey?

Choreographers take the fragments of a dance movement and connect them into flowing rhythms and patterns. They design and direct the dance. They imagine the dance as a whole, then identify and nurture each segment, merging them together with smooth transitions. But the dance isn't done yet—they rank, review, revise, rehearse and repeat.

Choreographers are the artists with the vision of what the performance will look like on the stage. They know the entire story, the themes that require emphasis so their meanings are clear to the audience.

They know every move, down to how high the elbows need to be in one segment to how the moves of each individual amplify the other dancers around him. Choreographers determine where faster or softer movements are needed. They show us the slow gestures that best correspond to what the story requires at that time.

A choreographer spends many hours on guiding the dancer, even down to small movements with the hands or eyes. He or she encourages and changes movements based on an individual's strengths and limitations and how that dancer's pacing and style best blends with others on the stage.

God is the choreographer in our dance. He will lead us in ranking our practices, then reviewing and revising the steps. He will be present as we rehearse our movements with him and remain with us as we repeat the spiritual patterns that draw us closer to him.

We are the dancers. Our ears are open. We learn. We prepare and practice. We mirror his movements.

Bring Our Best

As we listen to God as our Choreographer, we bring our BEST.

Choreographers often use four basic dance elements to create the entire dance routine. These elements are BEST — body, energy, space, and time. Creating our rule of life uses the BEST acronym too. Actually, I add a bonus too, some R's at the end. Is that a word? BESTRRRR?

Body

Gather the ideas from the last chapter and list the movements/practices that resonate with you and you think will be part of your rule. What elements from the ideas we learned last chapter appeal to you, stretch you? Tingle your imagination. Invite you inward. Write a list of all the things you do that nurture your spirit.

That list you create, whether or not you know it, is your unconscious rule of life. By recognizing those things, you do that are already spirit-filled, and by doing them more deliberately, you can make your unconscious rule of life into a conscious one.

Divide your list among the eight categories: seeking God, prayer, work, study, spiritual community and worship, care for your body, reaching out, and hospitality. Your initial list may leave some empty categories. Listen to your heart's desires when discerning your rule. God often speaks to us through our heart's desires. When and where do you feel closest to God? How do you enter most deeply into an awareness of God's love for you?

Make sure your rule includes some joy, play, and fun. Ask God for wisdom and to show you what to include and if this is the best season for this practice.

Take baby steps. Don't make your rule impossible to follow.

Baby steps are good, but give yourself a little bit of a challenge, too. What stretches your spirit?

Energy

Which practices give you energy? Get you excited? This step also invites you to think about the how of your rule? How will the pieces come together? Figure out how much structure you need: lots or just a little? Figure out how to help yourself be accountable for keeping your rule. See a spiritual director or talk with a spiritual friend about your rule regularly.

Try it out to sense the flow. Play with the movement. It's important to feel the music. What is your deepest desire as you grow closer to God? Is that yearning expressed in your rule?

Space

How will you create space for God and for others as you implement the practices on your list? Choose the specific steps. What is essential or mandatory for what you envision? Which ones can you improvise or revise later? Remember to keep it simple and aim for one page. The focus here is on being practical and realistic for yourself and your particular situation. It is quality, not quantity, that is sensible and useful. Simplicity is a key to success.

Where will you implement these practices? Imagine the sacred space surrounding you as you pray this framework. What would be the ideal environment for you to grow? You can dance on multiple stages and settings–how do you envision praying, serving, dancing with God in those spaces?

Time

When will you do these practices? Seek a balance of intentional time carved out of your daily schedule, such as morning devotional or yearly retreat, balancing these with spontaneous practices of pausing to look at God's creation in your backyard. Being present for the person right in front of you. Seeing God in detours and interruptions.

> *"It is unlikely that we will deepen our relationship with God in a casual or haphazard manner. There will be a need for some intentional commitment and some reorganization in our own lives. But there is nothing that will enrich our lives more than a deeper and clearer perception of God's presence in the routine of daily living."*
> William O. Paulsell

Prayerfully compile and study the various practices and desires that have been emerging.

There's no wrong way to do this. Set time aside for brainstorming with God. Consider every word and possibility and sense how you feel. Is it life giving? If you resist it, why are you feeling that way? Write out all ideas on paper or digitally and ponder the ideas. Put down even stray thoughts that you may add later or in a different season.

Once you see them on the list in its entirety, like the jigsaw puzzle discussed last chapter, the segments will merge and create an order for you. This is a step that may be helpful to experience with a spiritual director or mentor. Is that prayer practice really connecting with you? How does serving others form your faith? Look for the patterns and connections. Ruthlessly cross things out and commit yourself to the most important things.

In our preparation, besides bringing out BEST, a few "R's" also guide our insight.

Review and Revise
This step takes openness and willingness to change, to let go, to accept an area you may have ignored. I mentioned earlier I added the practice of hospitality to my rule even though it wasn't a strength, because God kept reminding me about its importance.

I have made notes throughout the years in the column next to this word as I grow deeper in this practice.

As you create the pattern within your rule this may be a good time to journal about your progress. Write your rule in longhand. How does that feel?

Discuss with God in the form of a dialog about how the dance is developing.

Share your rule with your spiritual director, your spouse, or a trusted friend. Listen to their feedback. Are you being realistic? Are you being gracious to yourself? Where are you challenging yourself?

Are there blind spots you're missing? Does this framework draw you closer to God?

Read your rule regularly. It is easy to forget the stuff we don't like so much. You're going to have trouble keeping a rule sometimes. Recognize that you're human and try again.

Rehearse and Repeat

Rehearsal contains a tiny word within its walls. HEAR.

Think about what you hear in a rehearsal hall.

"Let's repeat that movement again."
"One more time with more passion in this section."
"Let's take it slow through this line, then try it again at a normal pace."
"Keep going. You can do it."
"This isn't working. Let's step back and figure this out."
"Can I sing this at a different key?"

At its best, a rule of life is a fluid document. As you grow and change, so will it. Take ten minutes, maybe weekly or monthly, to check-in with yourself and look over your rule. What's working? What's not working? What can be tweaked? Maybe you do this check-in once a quarter or once a year. Set a reminder on your calendar. Don't forget to actually do it.

Dance is a beautiful art form that tells a story through patterns and movements. The choreographer creates the framework and leads the dancer towards the completion of a masterpiece.

The dancer listens intently to the music and responds to its speed, rhythm, and volume. Notice how God's voice directs and stirs your emotions. Listen to your heart to learn what you are yearning for now. Listening is key to creating your rule of life.

Find a place to be quiet and still and listen to God. Play with the ideas you previously gathered to add to your rule and invite God to show you how to rank them in the best order. Ask for vision to review and revise them as you practice your dance. Then practice, practice, practice–the rehearsal of the rule of life. Dance with God as your Choreographer.

Dancers learns a routine two or three steps/patterns/sequences at a time. Build your rule over time and the rhythm and beauty will emerge. The steps materialize into a dance. You will mirror the great Choreographer.

> *"How we spend our days is, of course, how we spend our lives."*
> *Annie Dillard*

Dancing with the Questions

1. Have you ever imagined God as the choreographer of your life before? How does that change your image of God and how you live?
2. What patterns are emerging in your rule of life? How will you use BESTRRRR?
3. Take a moment to assess that what you are creating is not too lengthy or complicated. Hold your initial rule lightly and seek God's guidance.

Prayer

Lord, my Choreographer, show me. Lead me. Help me hear from you in this rehearsal hall and practice the disciplines you are designing just for me. Open my eyes to see the patterns and to hear your insights as this rule of life emerges. Amen.

CHAPTER 7:
DIVINE DANCE PARTNER

Floor to ceiling mirrors line one wall in most dance studios. The mirrors aid in dance practice to provide feedback, to correct movements, and to assess if the dancer is in sync with the choreographer.

The dancer mirrors the steps of the instructor, not wandering away from the prescribed rhythms of the music framing the dance. Some dancers share that using the mirror while learning the patterns helps in the initial introduction to each step. Throughout practices the dancers then periodically return to face the mirror to fine-tune, enhance, and correct their movements.

The dancer desires a smooth rhythm. Practicing in front of a mirror aligns the dancer leading to consistent flow from one movement to another. They add small adjustments and may even add an innovative movement to a pattern.

> "I will instruct you and teach you the way you should go;
> I will counsel you with my eye upon you."
> Psalms 32: 8

What does it mean to partner with God?

My life verse is from Hebrews 12: 2: "fixing our eyes on Jesus, the pioneer and perfecter of faith." Repeating this verse and living it consistently helps me partner with God. I am not better or equal to God as a partner, but I follow God's lead, reflect his love, model his way.

What an honor it is, a gift, to come alongside with God, walking each day with the sacred, and learning from the Master.

Spending time with God becomes our mirror for our spiritual practice identified in the rule of life. Mirroring God's movement leads us to a SMOOTH dance rhythm in our patterns of daily dancing with him.

You've decided your rule of life, your framework, now how will you begin? SMOOTH is an easy way to partner intentionally with God in your rule of life.

SMOOTH stands for:

S – Start with the Sacred
M – Move slowly. Be gentle with yourself.
O – Observe, obey, and do the work
O – Obstacles
T – Time and place
H – Hold lightly the honor and hallow the process

Let's explore the meaning of SMOOTH in our spiritual practice.

S–Start with the Sacred

We acknowledge that God is the lead, the focal point, the very purpose of our desire to live a life with life-giving spiritual patterns. God is the one who gives us the framework and teaches us his way. We partner with God, not aiming for unattainable perfection, but for consistent practices.

The purpose of a rule of life is to live in rhythms that keep our hearts and minds centered on God. We focus on spiritual practices that support spending time with God and remind us who God is and that we are God's children.

We face the mirror following God's patterns of living by paying attention to God and the divine presence in our lives.

It is necessary to start our rule of life with God and keep the focus on God. This step may sound easy, but I have found my ego, the noise of the world, and temptations and distraction continually tangle my steps on rocky ground.

The practice of starting each day with God in praise and gratitude smooths my path and brings my steps back in alignment with our Creator. Don't forget to start daily with the Sacred.

M–Move slowly. Be gentle with yourself.

As you begin the dance, start slowly and be gentle with yourself. I hear my directees in spiritual direction sessions lament about imperfections, disappointment in themselves, and even anger toward their mistakes.

Too high expectations often lead to discouragement. Dancers practice, practice, practice many long hours, unseen by others, to learn the steps of the dance. Persistence, patience, and gentleness—all gifts of the Holy Spirit—are ours. This is a great time to ask for these gifts and unwrap them as you progress in applying your rule for living.

Starting any new habit, ritual, or practice takes time. Be gentle with yourself. Start over as needed. Make adjustments to the season in your life or unexpected circumstances.

Give yourself lots of time for the slow development of what works best for you. As you examine your life, you may notice many areas that need work. The best approach is to start with only one or two elements for the first few months. Then, after you experience some success with those, you will want to add another building block to your rule. Or you may want to stay with the same element to work on over a long period of time. Be willing to make mistakes, try again, and learn new things.

O—Observe, obey, and do the work

Be honest in your practice of your rule of life. Watch yourself. Listen quietly to God's nudges. Do the work God calls you to do.

This step develops spiritual muscle memory.

Just like the body enjoys doing and can learn repetitive movements, so does your spirit. Patterns become the building blocks we know and don't have to spend extra energy remembering. Building spiritual muscle memory takes time for the unfamiliar movements to become known deep inside our souls.

We can learn muscle memory skills by watching a one-year-old learn to walk. They watch others. With a slow and steady effort, they rise to their feet. They give themselves time to learn.

They wobble, fall down, and try again. They do the work over and over until soon they not only walk but run.

Researchers explain that long-term memory is stored in two different forms: declarative and non-declarative. Declarative is memory you can describe, find the words to write out or talk about. Memory begins here.

Non-declarative memory is harder to explain; it is more experienced. For example, you may know how to swim but can't necessarily explain it. Working out of this type of memory takes longer and is where the spiritual muscle memory is stored. The practice becomes ingrained more in the subconscious than the conscious. Dance moves from awkward and unnatural to mystical, smooth art.

Doing the work, the practice deepens within our soul, and our rules take root.

O–Obstacles

Expect some obstacles to arise when getting started with a rule of life. Old habits don't like to give up their power and new habits can be shy to step forward.

As you write and practice your rule of life, the ego takes its eyes off the Choreographer and onto what others are doing. The comparison game interrupts our practice. You may not feel like your rule is good enough. Not complete enough.

God is always enough and will help you with each step.

Another obstacle is not allowing enough time for the practice of your rule to develop. Don't be too quick to give up. Like any other skill, even like dancing, practice is the key.

Ask yourself if each rule you begin gives life. It is okay to tweak. To try something new. To come back at a later time to that step again. Maybe you weren't called to do the jive or jitterbug. Maybe you are more of a waltz person. Be honest and open to where God continues to lead you in this dance.

"Dance like nobody is watching" is good advice for this stage in practicing your rule. None of us want to look foolish, but we are beginners in this spiritual dance and far from perfect. Know your obstacles and work around them with God's help.

T–Time and place

This point of implementing your rule presents an opportunity to assess your time and place in this moment of life. What season are you in? What practices draw you closer to God right now, right here?

Remember the obstacle of not allowing enough time. I am a morning person, so many of my disciplines occur early in the day. But others find evening or just before bed a better choice. At the first of every year, I look at the calendar and schedule my yearly retreat. Some years are harder than others to find the right time and place, but I intentionally get that date sooner than later, so I don't forget or miss an opportunity.

Assess the place where you practice your rule. Do you need to print a copy of your rule and display in a place where you see it more often? I keep my rule in my Bible and another copy in my journal.

Maybe the place you try these new disciplines isn't the best place. Look around your house to see if another location may give you quiet, solitude, or an atmosphere for prayer and listening.

H–Hold lightly to your rule and honor and hallow the process. Remember this rule starts with God and the words are a gift from God. We don't cling to the rule, but allow it to sit lightly like a bird on a perch, in our hearts.

As you review SMOOTH, starting with the sacred, moving slowly and gently, observing and doing the work, aware of obstacles and how time and place form your practice, lifting your rule and presenting your intention to God invites the holy to enter this process.

I ask God to bless my rule every time I read it. I hold the paper with the written rules up with open palms into his grace and love. I know the present attempt to create how I think God is calling me to live isn't perfect, but I ask God to bless my intentions.

> *Collect for Guidance*
> *O God, by whom the meek are guided in judgment and light rises up in darkness for the godly: grant us, in all our doubts and uncertainties, the grace to ask what you would have us to do, that the spirit of wisdom may save us from all false choices, and that in your light we may see light, and in your straight path may not stumble, through Jesus Christ our Lord. Amen.*
> *Book of Common Prayer.*

At this point, I also ask God to help me hear his guidance and the beat of his music. I know deep listening for me requires stillness, silence, and solitude. I hear God in prayer, worship, and music, too. God nudges appear with serving and listening to others. A word or phrase from scripture resonates and almost demands to be written into my rule as part of its foundation.

Dancers understand the importance of beats, especially when learning new dance steps. Spiritual practices also have a natural ebb and flow. Dancers repeat some steps multiple times.

Listen to God. He will direct your ways.

> *You're blessed when you stay on course, walking steadily on the road revealed by God. You're blessed when you follow his directions, doing your best to find him. That's right—you don't go off on your own; you walk straight along the road he set. You, God, prescribed the right way to live; now you expect us to live it. Oh, that my steps might be steady, keeping to the course you set; Then I'd never have any regrets in comparing my life with your counsel. I*

thank you for speaking straight from your heart; I learn the pattern of your righteous ways. I'm going to do what you tell me to do; don't ever walk off and leave me. Psalm 119:1-8 The Message

Dancing with the Questions

1. Think back to a time you felt in step with God. What helped you know that? How would that help implement your rule of life?
2. Move slow was one step in this chapter and one many find difficult to do. How about you? How do you know when you are rushing ahead and need to slow down?
3. What obstacles have or could stop you from practicing your rule of life?
4. How will you honor and hallow your rule of life?

Prayer

Lord, I want to be in step with you. Mirroring you. Following you. I ask for wisdom as I dance with you and discover all you want me to be. Amen.

CHAPTER 8:
PRACTICE

We learn by practice. Whether it means to learn to dance by practicing dancing or to learn to live by practicing living, the principles are the same. One becomes in some area an athlete of God.
Martha Graham

Remember the story at the beginning of this book? How do you get to Carnegie Hall? Practice. Practice. Practice.

Practice is easy to say, to write about, and to preach, but it is much harder to implement. We have all been there. Trying to break a bad habit. Attempting to eat healthier and exercise daily. We vow we are going to do this new thing, yet two weeks later–poof–we forget, get distracted, or just plain give up.

Why do we need to practice? Research shows, on average, 80% of everything newly learned is forgotten. While you may feel confident with what you're learning, as soon as you leave, you can forget most of what you've gone over. But does this have to be the case? No. Studies further show that with frequent practice, one can keep much more. It is important to note that the key phrase is "frequent practice."

Practice comes with a heavy dose of perseverance. I love the image Martha Graham shared in the quote above — an athlete of God.

Being involved in a sport never has been part of my DNA. I am old enough to grow up in a time of only limited girls' sports in high schools and am so thankful that is no longer true.

My daughter excelled in track in her school days and I became an obsessive sports mom. An expert in the different events. A sideline coach recording times, how to line up properly, where to put your eyes before the start of each race. I studied proper nutrition and which type of fluids to bring along depending on the weather conditions. I searched for information about the best shoes to wear for the fastest time. Yes, my passion and preoccupation with her competition bordered on crazy.

I knew track, but I couldn't run. If it were me out there on the field, I would come in last every time. Ha, I probably couldn't even finish a race. I had the knowledge, but never practiced. Mental know-how isn't the same as skill. Practice is an essential step.

How do we become athletes of God? Implementing our rule of life is a significant step.

CREATING A RULE OF LIFE

Only be careful, and watch yourselves closely
so that you do not forget the things your eyes have seen
or let them fade from your heart as long as you live.
Teach them to your children and to their children after them.
Deuteronomy 4:9

Annie Bosler, in her TED video titled "How to Practice Effectively for Just About Anything" defines practice as the "repetition of an action with the goal of improvement and it helps us perform with more ease, speed, and confidence. Practice affects our brain."

Her research stressed how our brain works with two kinds of neural tissue — gray and white matter. Gray matter processes and directs the information that the brain takes in and the white matter conveys the information down the spinal cord throughout the body and heart through its fatty membrane called myelin that surrounds white matter like insulation. A recent study indicated that practice increased the diameter of myelin. The repetitive motion builds the layer of the myelin sheath, creating stronger pathways for the body to remember.

How long does this take? Of course, there is no magic number, and the amount is hugely debated. Psychologist Dr. Ericsson's research is perhaps the best-known theory that it requires at least ten years and/or 10,000 hours of deliberate practice to achieve an expert level of performance in any given domain–and with musicians, more like 15-25 years in order to attain an elite international level.

Many of us may be familiar with this number, but did you notice the tiny adjective just before the word practice? Deliberate.

To be effective, practice involves repetition and constituency, is highly focused and takes in considering what we are doing and our limitations. Of course, this does not include mindless trial and error, but an active plan of action to reach for the end results we are seeking.

Practice our rule of life – finding just that right rhythm - takes time and giving ourselves grace when we fail. I find following Three R's of Practice helps me in applying this step in our dance with God.

The Three R's of Practice

In school, we learned the three r's—reading, 'riting (writing), and 'rithmetic (arithmetic)—as the foundation of our studies. In dancing to divine rhythms, the three R's of practicing our rule of life are:

- Realistic and repetitive schedule
- Reminders
- Release

First, review your rule of life. To do everything you have written perfectly right from the start is not realistic. Begin small. What are you already doing and will find easy to maintain in your present season of life? What one item could you add to the mix? How often do you want to add a new practice? Weekly? Monthly? Quarterly?

Deliberate practicing is the implementation of that behavior we are working on and is built upon repetition. Remember you are creating layers of myelin sheaths in your body. This will take time and hitting that repeat button multiple times.

Repeat it in your mind, as well as with your body. When you are open to seeing yourself practicing these disciplines, sensing how you will feel and grow, hearing God inviting you into his music, practicing becomes easier.

No matter what else you do, repetition is a must. Repetition reduces the time between when you think of doing something and when you do it. With this, there is no undue effort to remember, which can hinder the flow of your dancing. Repetition aids in recalling things you have learned, avoiding their forgetfulness.

Though Mozart was a child prodigy, did you know he didn't write his first masterpiece until he was 21 years of age? He spent the previous 18 years studying music and practicing. While an extraordinary composer and musician, his success wasn't achieved through his talents alone. It required much practice and dedication.

A realistic schedule also supports practice. It is far better to slowly build up your practices in your rule of life rather than trying to do all of them at once. Take an honest look at what will work for you at this present time. Ask God for insight into how much to try and what to leave for another time.

Practice is then framed with this second step: reminders. Habits form best when tied to an existing habit. For example, when I enter my prayer space, I light a candle — a first step in quieting my soul, preparing to listen to God. Many days I set an alarm on my smartphone to remind me to take a prayer pause midafternoon and evening.

Release is the last step.

Releasing what comes from our practice into God's hands and allowing space for his guidance will resolve and clarify our rule of life. At times, I cling too tightly to what I plan, what I want, and what I think is best.

Quiet listening to the Dance Instructor and being willing to try again and to practice new ways increases my stamina and the beauty of my rhythms. Letting go of my ego, my to-do list, my eagerness to "do things right by following a strict law" often leads to discouragement in my practices.

Release brings relaxation. I ease into my Dance Partner's arms and mirror His steps. This image reminds me to surrender and follow.

Insightful Dance Story

The following is an intriguing dance story shared on the Washington National Cathedral website. Its words reminded me of the importance to persevere in practicing the discipline that opens my heart to align my life with God.

The Russian Ballerina

There was a young Russian girl who had a dream of becoming a famous ballet dancer in a great dance company. She had lessons in her town and worked hard. When she was old enough, she decided to audition for the biggest ballet company in Moscow.

The auditions were divided into two segments. There was a first audition and a second audition one month later for those that were not accepted at the first, similar to a Re-dance in a dancesport competition. The purpose of the second audition was for a B Company (second level) since the first-picks were accepted already.

After many days of practicing and hard work, the young dancer arrived in Moscow for the audition. She was motivated and scared at the same time. The judge panel was made up of the best ballet teachers in Russia, including the world-renowned director of the company. When they called her name, she was given a chance to show her routine and skills.

After her performance, the director stood up and said, "Thanks dear, for coming and for your performance. However, I think I can talk for all of the judges on the panel when I say that your level is far from what we are looking for, for our company. You are not good enough for us. Actually, let me add something and give you my personal opinion, my dear. I do not think that you were made to dance. I advise you to look for another art but not dance. The second audition is in one month, but if I were you, I would not come."

This was a tremendous shock for the ballet dancer. She knew that the audition would be a challenge, but she would have never expected that she would be told to stop dancing.

Yet this ballerina had one trait that differentiated her from the other dancers. She had an internal voice telling her that none of what the director had said was true, that she was a talented dancer, and that she could do even better. Deciding to try again one month later, she decided that even if she would not be accepted, at least she would have given it her all. She would not go home and give up as soon as the first barrier presented itself.

When she arrived for the second audition one month later, the director saw her and immediately said, "Hi, my dear. Do you remember what I told you one month ago?"

The girl said yes.

"So," continued the director, "why did you come back?"

At this point, the young dancer was shaking. She took a deep breath and said, "I came back because I don't believe that I was not made for dance. That may be your opinion, but I do not accept that as my reality. I truly believe that I can learn fast and that I will be a professional. What you said to me was your personal judgment and I don't accept that as something that I am."

The director stood up with a big smile and said, "Do you know one thing, my dear? What I told you last month was the exact response that I gave to all of the girls that auditioned. I advised them to go home and forget about being a ballet dancer. And do you know why I did that?"

The young girl was shocked. She shook her head in confusion.

The director continued, "Because if you want to be a great dancer, I can teach you all the techniques and routines. I can teach you anything you need to know. However, to survive in this stressful and sometimes unfair ballet world, I need to have mentally tough dancers in my company. I need to have artists with great personalities who are focused, that believe in themselves, and won't break down with the challenges and adversities of this profession. I am looking for dancers that will come back for the second audition and tell me, 'No, I am better than that, that is just your opinion, but I believe that I can be a great dancer'. And let me tell you one other thing. You don't need to show me your routine today, because you are already accepted into my company. Congratulations!"

God invites us to dance. Now I don't believe God is like this dance director, only inviting a few and rejecting and discouraging others. All of us are invited to dance. God waits, urging us closer to hear his heartbeat and to move to his rhythms. We just need to keep showing up, entering the dance conservatory, and practice, practice, practice.

A Rule of Life Blessing

May you hear God as you write a rhythm of life.
May God light your way and reveal a path forward.
May you discover deep desires and values to express in words.
May you see the sacredness of this work and its importance.
May courage lead you deeper consistently.
May you realize the uniqueness of your journey and enjoy its gifts.
May you long for the One who longs for you.
May you experience grace and forgiveness as you travel along this way.
And may you know God and dance with the Divine forever.

RESOURCES

- I invite you to visit my blog – https://healthyspirituality.org where I write frequently on spiritual practices such as a rule of life. Please check it out and subscribe.

- Books you may find helpful:

  Soul Feast by Marjorie Thompson–has a great chapter on writing a Rule of Life in her newly revised edition.

  Living Faith Day by Day–Debra K. Farrington

  At Home in the World–a Rule of Life for the Rest of Us–Margaret Guenther

  Crafting a Rule of Life by Steve Macchia–wonderful complete resource

- Internet resources:

    www.Ssje.org/growrule–a PDF about rule of life to download at no cost.

    http://www.cslewisinstitute.org/webfm_send/338–interesting paper about rule of life.

    Crafting a Rule of Life website–http://www.ruleoflife.com–resources and examples

    https://sacredordinarydays.com/pages/rule-of-life

    https://renovare.org/articles/rule-of-life-six-streams

ABOUT THE AUTHOR

Jean Wise is a writer, speaker, retreat leader, and spiritual director. She is a contributing author of devotions for four compilations published by Barbour, plus solo author of *Let Every Heart Prepare Him Room, an Advent Devotion* by Barbour Books.

Other books by Jean are:

Sacred Surroundings: Finding Grace in Every Place

Spiritual Retreats: A Guide to Slowing Down to be with God

Whispers: Being with God in Breath Prayers

Fuel Your Faith: A Practical Guide to Igniting a Healthy Spirituality

40 Voices: A Lenten Devotional

Christmas Crossroads: 30 Devotionals for the Holiday Season

The Communicator's Companion: Devotionals for Speakers and Writers

Upcoming: *WWW – Reflections of God's Wonder, Wisdom and Whimsey*

One of the best gifts you can give to an author is a review of her books. Please take the time, not to just for me, but for all the writers you read – please, write a review!

Jean is a Deacon for her church, facilitating faith formation and an active spiritual direction practice. She is a frequent speaker for gatherings and retreats in northwest Ohio. She writes weekly on her blog, www.healthyspirituality.org.

Jean is a RN with her Masters in Nursing. She retired from public health in 2006 to focus on speaking and writing ministry. She has discovered her calling to nurture others - as she practiced in nursing and now as she helps others grow closer to God in her ministry of spiritual direction, writing and speaking.

Besides her blog you can connect with Jean online at:

Facebook: https://www.facebook.com/Jeanwiseauthor
Pinterest https://www.pinterest.com/jeanwise22
Instagram: https://www.instagram.com/jeanwise/

A very special thank you to Janet Hitchcock for all her encouragement, prayers, and wonderful editing.

www.ingramcontent.com/pod-product-compliance
Lightning Source LLC
Chambersburg PA
CBHW061339040426
42444CB00011B/2993